GW01046824

contents

Please note that Australian cup and
spoon measurements are metric.
A conversion chart appears on page 62.

2 **butter** up

Indulgent and scrumptious, these sweet butters will transform warm muffins from the merely delectable to the positively heavenly! Each recipe makes about 1 cup – enough for 12 muffins (or six large muffins).

citrus liqueur butter

125g butter

2 teaspoons finely grated orange rind

2 teaspoons Grand Marnier

1 cup (160g) icing sugar mixture

Beat butter, rind and liqueur in small bowl with electric mixer until as pale as possible. Gradually beat in icing sugar.

Per tablespoon 8.6g fat; 547kJ

maple syrup butter

125g butter

1 tablespoon maple-flavoured syrup

2/3 cup (110g) icing sugar mixture

Beat butter and syrup in small bowl with electric mixer until as pale as possible. Gradually beat in icing sugar.

Per tablespoon 8.6g fat; 488kJ

cinnamon honey butter

125g butter

1 tablespoon honey

1/2 teaspoon ground cinnamon

2/3 cup (110g) icing sugar mixture

Beat butter, honey and cinnamon in small bowl with electric mixer until as pale as possible. Gradually beat in icing sugar.

Per tablespoon 8.6g fat; 496kJ

vanilla butter

125g butter

1 teaspoon vanilla essence

1 cup (160g) icing sugar mixture

Beat butter and essence in small bowl with electric mixer until as pale as possible. Gradually beat in icing sugar.

Per tablespoon 8.5g fat; 534kJ

4

lime syrup
coconut muffins

2¹/₂ cups (375g)
self-raising flour

1 cup (90g)
desiccated coconut

1 cup (220g)
caster sugar

1 tablespoon finely
grated lime rind

1 cup (250ml)
buttermilk

125g butter, melted

2 eggs

lime syrup

¹/₂ cup (110g)
caster sugar

¹/₄ cup (60ml) water

2 teaspoons finely
grated lime rind

¹/₃ cup (80ml)
lime juice

Preheat oven to moderately hot. Grease 12-hole (¹/₃ cup/80ml) muffin pan.

Combine flour, coconut and sugar in large bowl; stir in combined remaining ingredients.

Spoon mixture into prepared pan. Bake in moderately hot oven about 20 minutes.

Transfer muffins to wire rack over tray; pour hot lime syrup over hot muffins. Drain syrup from tray and pour over muffins again.

Lime Syrup Combine ingredients in small saucepan; stir over heat, without boiling, until sugar dissolves. Simmer, uncovered, without stirring, 2 minutes.

MAKES 12
Per serving 15.1g fat; 1506kJ

6 apple buttermilk muffins
with coconut crumble

2¹/₂ cups (375g)
self-raising flour

³/₄ cup (150g) firmly
packed brown sugar

1 teaspoon
ground cinnamon

410g can pie apples

1 egg

²/₃ cup (160ml)
buttermilk

¹/₂ cup (125ml)
vegetable oil

coconut crumble

¹/₄ cup (35g) plain flour

1¹/₂ tablespoons
caster sugar

¹/₂ cup (25g)
flaked coconut

20g butter

Preheat oven to moderately hot. Grease
12-hole (¹/₃ cup/80ml) muffin pan.
Combine flour, sugar and cinnamon in large
bowl; stir in apple, then combined egg,
buttermilk and oil. Spoon mixture into prepared
pan; top with coconut crumble. Bake in
moderately hot oven about 20 minutes.
Coconut Crumble Place ingredients in small
bowl; rub butter into mixture using fingertips.

MAKES 12
Per serving 11.8g fat; 1130kJ

white chocolate and
macadamia muffins

*2 cups (300g)
self-raising flour*

*²/₃ cup (150g)
caster sugar*

*³/₄ cup (140g)
white Choc Bits*

*¹/₂ cup (75g)
coarsely chopped
macadamias, toasted*

60g butter, melted

³/₄ cup (180ml) milk

1 egg, beaten lightly

Preheat oven to moderately hot. Grease six-hole (³/₄ cup/180ml) muffin pan.
Combine ingredients in large bowl; mix well. Spoon mixture into prepared pan. Bake in moderately hot oven about 25 minutes.

MAKES 6
Per serving 28g fat; 2442kJ

almond muffins

2¹/₂ cups (375g)
self-raising flour

1 teaspoon
ground nutmeg

1 cup (80g) flaked
almonds, toasted

³/₄ cup (165g)
caster sugar

1 egg

1¹/₄ cups (310ml) milk

90g butter, melted

¹/₂ cup (160g) apricot jam

Preheat oven to
moderate. Grease
12-hole (¹/₃ cup/80ml)
muffin pan.
Combine flour, nutmeg,
nuts and sugar in large
bowl; stir in combined
egg, milk and butter.
Spoon half of the muffin
mixture into prepared
pan, make a well in each
muffin, spoon in rounded
teaspoons of jam; top with
remaining muffin mixture.
Bake in moderate oven
about 30 minutes.

MAKES 12
Per serving
11.7g fat; 1291kJ

citrus coconut muffins

2¹/₂ cups (375g)
self-raising flour

1 cup (220g)
caster sugar

90g butter,
chopped coarsely

2 teaspoons finely
grated lemon rind

2 teaspoons finely
grated orange rind

1 egg, beaten lightly

³/₄ cup (180ml) milk

¹/₄ cup (15g)
shredded coconut

Preheat oven to
moderately hot. Grease
12-hole (¹/₃ cup/80ml)
muffin pan.
Combine flour and sugar
in large bowl; rub in
butter. Add combined
rinds, egg and milk.
Spoon mixture into
prepared pan; sprinkle
with coconut, press
coconut on gently.
Bake in moderately hot
oven about 25 minutes.

MAKES 12
Per serving 8.4g fat; 1065kJ

10 ginger date muffins
with caramel sauce

1 cup (160g) coarsely
chopped seeded dates

1/3 cup (80ml) water

1/4 teaspoon
bicarbonate of soda

2 cups (300g)
self-raising flour

1 cup (150g)
plain flour

2 teaspoons
ground ginger

1/2 teaspoon
mixed spice

1 cup (200g) firmly
packed brown sugar

2 teaspoons finely
grated orange rind

1 egg, beaten lightly

1¼ cups (310ml) milk

1/4 cup (60ml)
vegetable oil

caramel sauce

1 cup (200g) firmly
packed brown sugar

1 cup (250ml) cream

40g butter

Preheat oven to moderately hot. Grease 12-hole (1/3 cup/80ml) muffin pan.

Combine dates and the water in medium saucepan, bring to a boil. Remove from heat, add soda; stand 5 minutes.

Sift dry ingredients into large bowl; stir in date mixture and remaining ingredients. Spoon mixture into prepared pan.

Bake in moderately hot oven about 20 minutes. Serve warm with caramel sauce.

Caramel Sauce Combine ingredients in medium saucepan; stir over heat, without boiling, until sugar dissolves. Simmer, without stirring, for about 3 minutes or until thickened slightly.

MAKES 12
Per serving 18.4g fat; 1929kJ

chocolate

honeycomb muffins

2 cups (300g)
self-raising flour

1/4 cup (55g)
caster sugar

1 cup (190g) white
Choc Bits

100g chocolate-
coated honeycomb,
chopped coarsely

1 egg, beaten lightly

60g butter, melted

1 cup (250ml)
buttermilk

1/4 cup (90g) honey

1 teaspoon
vanilla essence

Preheat oven to moderately hot. Grease
12-hole (1/3 cup/80ml) muffin pan.
Combine flour, sugar, Choc Bits and honeycomb
in large bowl; stir in combined remaining
ingredients. Spoon mixture into prepared pan.
Bake in moderately hot oven about 20 minutes.

MAKES 12
Per serving 11.9g fat; 1255kJ

low-fat wholemeal

raspberry lemon muffins

*2 cups (320g)
wholemeal
self-raising flour*

*1/2 cup (75g) white
self-raising flour*

*1/2 teaspoon
bicarbonate of soda*

*3/4 cup (165g)
caster sugar*

*2 teaspoons finely
grated lemon rind*

2 eggs

*1 cup (250ml)
skim milk*

*1/4 cup (60ml)
vegetable oil*

125g fresh raspberries

*1/4 cup (20g)
flaked almonds*

Preheat oven to moderately hot. Grease
10 holes (1/3 cup/80ml) of muffin pan.
Sift flours, soda and sugar into large bowl;
stir in rind, combined eggs, milk and oil, then
raspberries. Spoon mixture into prepared pan;
sprinkle with nuts. Bake in moderately hot
oven about 25 minutes.

MAKES 10
Per serving 8.8g fat; 1186kJ

chocolate
rum 'n' raisin muffins

1 cup (170g) raisins, chopped finely

¼ cup (60ml) dark rum

2½ cups (375g) self-raising flour

½ cup (50g) cocoa powder

1 cup (200g) firmly packed brown sugar

150g dark chocolate, chopped finely

2 eggs

125g butter, melted

1 cup (250ml) buttermilk

Preheat oven to moderately hot. Grease 12-hole (⅓ cup/80ml) muffin pan.

Place raisins and rum in small bowl; stand 10 minutes.

Sift flour and cocoa into large bowl; stir in sugar and chocolate, then raisin mixture and combined eggs, butter and buttermilk. Spoon mixture into prepared pan. Bake in moderately hot oven about 20 minutes.

MAKES 12
Per serving 15.1g fat; 1675kJ

16 blueberry muffins

2 cups (300g)
self-raising flour

3/4 cup (150g) firmly
packed brown sugar

1 cup (150g) fresh or
frozen blueberries

1 egg

3/4 cup (180ml)
buttermilk

1/2 cup (125ml)
vegetable oil

Preheat oven to
moderately hot.
Grease six-hole
(3/4 cup/180ml)
muffin pan.
Combine flour, sugar
and blueberries
in large bowl; stir in
combined remaining
ingredients. Spoon
mixture into
prepared pan.
Bake in moderately
hot oven about
20 minutes.

MAKES 6
Per serving
21.3g fat; 1980kJ

date and **bran** muffins

These muffins can be made on the same day but will be much nicer if the mixture is refrigerated overnight and muffins are baked the following day.

1¼ cups (185g) plain flour

1 teaspoon bicarbonate of soda

1 teaspoon ground cinnamon

½ cup (110g) caster sugar

1¾ cups (105g) wheat bran

¾ cup (120g) finely chopped seeded dates

½ cup (125ml) vegetable oil

1½ cups (375ml) buttermilk

1 egg, beaten lightly

Sift flour, soda, cinnamon and sugar into large bowl; mix in bran and dates. Stir in remaining ingredients. Cover; refrigerate overnight. **Preheat** oven to moderately hot. Grease 12-hole (⅓ cup/80ml) muffin pan. Spoon mixture into prepared pan. **Bake** in moderately hot oven about 20 minutes.

MAKES 12
Per serving
11.3g fat; 1002kJ

18 fruity muffins

1 cup (190g)
mixed dried fruit

2 cups (500ml)
boiling water

3 cups (450g)
self-raising flour

1 cup (220g)
caster sugar

125g butter,
chopped coarsely

1/2 cup (125ml)
evaporated milk

2 eggs

Preheat oven to
moderately hot. Grease
12-hole (1/3 cup/80ml)
muffin pan.
Place fruit and the water
in medium bowl; stand
30 minutes, drain well.
Combine flour and sugar
in large bowl; rub in
butter. Stir in fruit and
combined milk and eggs.
Spoon mixture
into prepared pan.
Bake in moderately hot
oven about 20 minutes.

MAKES 12
Per serving
10.9g fat; 1434kJ

pear muffins

425g can pear halves in light syrup

2 cups (300g) self-raising flour

1/4 teaspoon ground cardamom

1/2 cup (75g) finely chopped macadamias

2 eggs

3/4 cup (180ml) cream

1/3 cup (80ml) maple-flavoured syrup

60g butter, melted

2 teaspoons raw sugar

Preheat oven to moderately hot. Grease 12-hole (1/3 cup/80ml) muffin pan.

Drain pears, pat dry on absorbent paper; chop pears finely. Combine flour, cardamom, pears and nuts in large bowl; stir in combined eggs, cream, syrup and butter. Spoon mixture into prepared pan, sprinkle with sugar. Bake in moderately hot oven about 20 minutes.

MAKES 12

Per serving 16.6g fat; 1156kJ

20 pecan
and coffee muffins

1¼ cups (125g) pecans

1½ cups (330g) caster sugar

¼ cup (60ml) water

2½ cups (375g) self-raising flour

90g butter, chopped coarsely

1¼ cups (310ml) buttermilk

1 egg

2 teaspoons dry instant coffee

coffee cream

185g packaged cream cheese

¼ cup (55g) caster sugar

1 teaspoon dry instant coffee

2 teaspoons boiling water

Preheat oven to moderately hot. Grease six-hole (¾ cup/180ml) muffin pan.

Reserve 12 whole nuts. Chop remaining nuts finely, sprinkle chopped nuts on greased oven tray.

Combine ½ cup of the sugar with the water in medium saucepan; stir over heat, without boiling, until sugar dissolves. Boil, uncovered, without stirring, about 10 minutes or until toffee is golden brown. Dip whole nuts into toffee using a fork, place on greased oven tray. Pour remaining toffee over chopped nuts, stir quickly until all nuts are covered in toffee; stand until set. Reserve whole nuts; chop remaining nut mixture finely.

Place flour in large bowl; rub in butter. Stir in remaining sugar and chopped nut mixture, then combined buttermilk, egg and coffee. Spoon mixture into prepared pan. Bake in moderately hot oven about 20 minutes. Serve cold muffins drizzled with coffee cream and topped with reserved whole nuts.

Coffee Cream Beat cheese, sugar and combined coffee and water in small bowl until smooth.

MAKES 6
Per serving 40.2g fat; 3590kJ

gluten-, dairy- and egg-free banana muffins

You will need about two large overripe bananas (460g) for this recipe.

1 cup (150g) brown rice flour

1/3 cup (40g) soy flour

2 teaspoons gluten-free baking powder

1/2 teaspoon mixed spice

1/2 teaspoon ground cinnamon

1 cup (95g) rice bran

1/3 cup (75g) firmly packed brown sugar

1 cup mashed bananas

1/2 cup (80g) sultanas

1/2 cup (75g) finely chopped dried apricots

60g dairy-free margarine, melted

1 cup (250ml) soy milk

Preheat oven to moderately hot. Grease 12-hole (1/3 cup/80ml) muffin pan with a little dairy-free margarine.

Sift flours, baking powder and spices into large bowl; stir in remaining ingredients. Spoon mixture into prepared pan. Bake in moderately hot oven about 25 minutes.

MAKES 12

Per serving 16.7g fat; 1232kJ

lemon

and poppy seed muffins

3 teaspoons finely grated lemon rind

1 cup (220g) caster sugar

2¼ cups (335g) self-raising flour

2 tablespoons poppy seeds

⅓ cup (80ml) lemon juice

1 egg, beaten lightly

1 cup (250ml) milk

60g butter, melted

Preheat oven to moderately hot. Grease 12-hole (⅓ cup/80ml) muffin pan.

Reserve 2 teaspoons of the rind and 2 tablespoons of the sugar.

Place flour in large bowl; stir in seeds and remaining sugar. Stir in remaining rind with juice, egg, milk and butter. Spoon mixture into prepared pan, sprinkle with combined reserved rind and sugar. Bake in moderately hot oven about 20 minutes.

MAKES 12
Per serving 6.5g fat; 970kJ

24 date muffins with
cinnamon frosting

¾ cup (120g) coarsely
chopped seeded dates

¼ cup (60ml) water

¼ teaspoon
bicarbonate of soda

1½ cups (225g) white
self-raising flour

1 cup (160g)
wholemeal
self-raising flour

1 teaspoon
mixed spice

¾ cup (150g) firmly
packed brown sugar

1 egg, beaten lightly

1 cup (250ml)
buttermilk

½ cup (125ml)
vegetable oil

cinnamon frosting

90g packaged
cream cheese

90g butter

1 cup (160g) icing
sugar mixture

1 teaspoon
ground cinnamon

Preheat oven to moderately
hot. Grease 12-hole
(⅓ cup/80ml) muffin pan.
Combine dates and the
water in small saucepan,
bring to a boil. Remove
from heat, add soda;
stand 5 minutes.
Sift dry ingredients into large
bowl; stir in date mixture
and remaining ingredients.
Spoon mixture into prepared
pan. Bake in moderately
hot oven about 20 minutes.
Spread top of cold muffins
with cinnamon frosting.
Cinnamon Frosting Beat
cheese and butter in small
bowl with electric mixer
until as white as possible.
Gradually beat in combined
icing sugar and cinnamon.

MAKES 12
Per serving 19.7g fat; 1636kJ

coffee # hazelnut
muffins

2 cups (300g)
self-raising flour

³/₄ cup (110g)
plain flour

¹/₃ cup (35g)
hazelnut meal

1 cup (200g) firmly
packed brown sugar

1¹/₂ tablespoons dry
instant coffee

1 tablespoon
boiling water

2 tablespoons Nutella

2 eggs, beaten lightly

1¹/₂ cups (375ml)
buttermilk

³/₄ cup (180ml)
vegetable oil

hazelnut frosting

1 cup (160g) icing
sugar mixture

1 tablespoon
cocoa powder

2 tablespoons Nutella

40g butter, softened

1 tablespoon milk

Preheat oven to moderately hot. Grease
12-hole (¹/₃ cup/80ml) muffin pan.
Sift flours into large bowl; stir in hazelnut
meal, sugar, combined coffee and water,
and remaining ingredients. Spoon mixture
into prepared pan. Bake in moderately hot
oven about 20 minutes. Spread cold muffins
with hazelnut frosting.
Hazelnut Frosting Sift icing sugar and cocoa
into small bowl; stir in remaining ingredients.

MAKES 12
Per serving 22.5g fat; 1931kJ

pumpkin,

pineapple and raisin muffins

2¹/₂ cups (375g) self-raising flour

1 cup (220g) caster sugar

1 cup (100g) finely grated uncooked butternut pumpkin

4 rings canned pineapple in natural juice, drained, chopped finely

¹/₂ cup (85g) finely chopped raisins

¹/₄ cup (60ml) cream

¹/₂ cup (125ml) vegetable oil

2 eggs

Preheat oven to moderately hot. Grease 12-hole (¹/₃ cup/80ml) muffin pan.
Combine flour, sugar, pumpkin, pineapple and raisins in large bowl; stir in combined remaining ingredients. Spoon mixture into prepared pan. Bake in moderately hot oven about 20 minutes.

MAKES 12
Per serving 13.1g fat; 1349kJ

chocolate orange

dessert muffins

2 cups (300g)
self-raising flour

1/2 cup (50g)
cocoa powder

1 1/4 cups (275g)
caster sugar

125g butter, melted

3/4 cup (180ml)
buttermilk

1 egg, beaten lightly

2 tablespoons
Grand Marnier

2 teaspoons finely
grated orange rind

12 (120g) chocolate
orange thins

crème anglaise

4 egg yolks

1/2 cup (110g)
caster sugar

1 2/3 cups (410ml) milk

Preheat oven to moderately hot. Grease
12-hole (1/3 cup/80ml) muffin pan.

Sift flour, cocoa and sugar into large bowl;
stir in butter, buttermilk, egg, liqueur and
rind. Spoon mixture into prepared pan. Break
each chocolate into three or four pieces, push
chocolate into each muffin. Make sure that
chocolate does not touch sides of muffin pan
and that mixture almost covers the chocolate.
Bake in moderately hot oven about 20 minutes.
Serve muffins with crème anglaise.

Crème Anglaise Beat egg yolks and sugar in
small bowl with electric mixer until thick and
pale. Pour milk into small saucepan, bring to a
boil, whisk milk into yolk mixture. Return mixture
to pan; stir over heat, without boiling, until
mixture thickens and coats back of spoon.

MAKES 12

Per serving 16.1g fat; 1759kJ

overnight date
and muesli muffins

These muffins can be made and baked on the same day but will be much nicer if the mixture is refrigerated overnight and muffins are baked the following day.

1¼ cups (185g)
plain flour

1¼ cups (160g)
toasted muesli

1 teaspoon ground
cinnamon

1 teaspoon
bicarbonate of soda

½ cup (100g) firmly
packed brown sugar

½ cup (30g)
wheat bran

¾ cup (120g) coarsely
chopped seeded dates

1½ cups (375ml)
buttermilk

½ cup (125ml)
vegetable oil

1 egg, beaten lightly

Combine ingredients in large bowl. Cover; refrigerate overnight.
Preheat oven to moderately hot. Grease 12-hole (⅓ cup/80ml) muffin pan. Spoon mixture into prepared pan. Bake in moderately hot oven about 25 minutes.

MAKES 12
Per serving 12.3g fat; 1155kJ

chocolate
cherry muffins

1 cup (150g)
self-raising flour

1/2 cup (75g) plain flour

1/2 cup (50g)
cocoa powder

1/2 teaspoon
bicarbonate of soda

1 cup (220g)
caster sugar

1/2 cup (45g)
desiccated coconut

1/2 cup (70g)
crushed nuts

1/2 cup (125g)
coarsely chopped
red glacé cherries

1/2 cup (95g) dark
Choc Bits

1 egg, beaten lightly

20g butter, melted

1/2 cup (125ml) milk

1/2 cup (125ml)
boiling water

Preheat oven to moderately hot. Grease
12-hole (1/3 cup/80ml) muffin pan.
Sift flours, cocoa and soda into large bowl;
stir in remaining ingredients. Spoon mixture
into prepared pan. Bake in moderately hot
oven about 20 minutes.

MAKES 12
Per serving 11g fat; 1241kJ

Short on time does not have to mean short on taste. These delicious muffins were baked in a 900-watt microwave oven.

pumpkin pecan muffins

You will need to cook about 300g pumpkin for this recipe.

1½ cups (225g) self-raising flour

½ teaspoon ground cinnamon

½ teaspoon mixed spice

⅓ cup (75g) firmly packed brown sugar

⅓ cup (80ml) vegetable oil

2 eggs, beaten lightly

¾ cup mashed cooked pumpkin

¾ cup (60ml) cream

¾ cup (90g) finely chopped pecans

Grease two six-hole (⅓ cup/80ml) microwave-safe muffin pans or line with paper muffin cases.

Combine flour, spices, sugar, oil, eggs, pumpkin, cream and ½ cup of the nuts in large bowl. Spoon mixture into prepared pans; sprinkle with remaining nuts.

Cook one pan at a time, uncovered, on MEDIUM-HIGH (70%) about 4 minutes or until muffins are just cooked. Stand 1 minute before turning muffins onto wire rack.

Makes 12
Per serving 14.9g fat; 973kJ

choc apricot muffins

1 cup (150g) dried apricots, chopped coarsely

2 cups (500ml) boiling water

1½ cups (225g) self-raising flour

⅓ cup (75g) firmly packed brown sugar

1 egg, beaten lightly

½ cup (125ml) vegetable oil

½ cup (125ml) milk

½ cup (95g) dark Choc Bits

Grease two six-hole (⅓ cup/80ml) microwave-safe muffin pans or line with paper muffin cases.
Place apricots and water in medium heatproof bowl; stand 5 minutes. Drain apricots, dry with absorbent paper. Reserve 2 tablespoons apricots. Place flour and sugar in large bowl; stir in remaining apricots with remaining ingredients. Spoon mixture into prepared pans; top with reserved apricots.
Cook one pan at a time, uncovered, on MEDIUM-HIGH (70%) about 4 minutes or until muffins are just cooked. Stand 1 minute before turning muffins onto wire rack.

Makes 12
Per serving 13.1g fat; 1040kJ

34 white chocolate and **berry** muffins

2 cups (300g) self-raising flour

2/3 cup (150g) caster sugar

2/3 cup (120g) finely chopped white chocolate

1 egg

3/4 cup (180ml) buttermilk

125g butter, melted

1 teaspoon vanilla essence

1/2 cup (75g) frozen raspberries

1/2 cup (75g) frozen blueberries

Preheat oven to moderately hot. Grease
12-hole (1/3 cup/80ml) muffin pan.
Combine flour, sugar and chocolate in large
bowl. Stir in combined egg, buttermilk, butter
and essence. Spoon mixture into prepared
pan; top with berries, press down gently.
Bake in moderately hot oven about 20 minutes.
Serve dusted with sifted icing sugar, if desired.

MAKES 12
Per serving 12.9g fat; 1195kJ

blackberry
streusel muffins

2 cups (300g)
self-raising flour

1¼ cups (170g)
frozen blackberries

1 medium (150g)
apple, peeled,
grated coarsely

¾ cup (150g) firmly
packed brown sugar

3 eggs, beaten lightly

⅓ cup (80ml)
vegetable oil

⅓ cup (80ml)
buttermilk

streusel topping

⅓ cup (50g) plain flour

2 tablespoons
brown sugar

1 teaspoon
mixed spice

30g butter

Preheat oven to moderately hot. Grease
12-hole (⅓ cup/80ml) muffin pan.
Place flour in large bowl; stir in remaining
ingredients. Spoon mixture into prepared pan.
Coarsely grate streusel topping over muffins.
Bake in moderately hot oven about 20 minutes.
Streusel Topping Combine flour, sugar and spice
in small bowl; rub in butter. Roll mixture into a
ball, wrap in plastic wrap, freeze until
firm enough to grate.

MAKES 12
Per serving 10.1g fat; 1080kJ

plum and pecan
wholemeal muffins

¹/₂ x 825g can plums in natural juice, drained

1 cup (150g) self-raising flour

²/₃ cup (100g) wholemeal self-raising flour

¹/₂ teaspoon mixed spice

¹/₄ teaspoon ground cinnamon

90g butter, chopped coarsely

¹/₃ cup (75g) raw sugar

¹/₂ cup (60g) coarsely chopped pecans

¹/₂ cup (125ml) milk

1 egg, beaten lightly

1 tablespoon raw sugar, extra

¹/₄ teaspoon ground cinnamon, extra

Preheat oven to moderately hot. Grease six-hole (³/₄ cup/180ml) muffin pan.

Drain plums, stand on absorbent paper for 10 minutes. Discard plum seeds, chop flesh coarsely.

Sift flours and spices into large bowl; rub in butter. Stir in plums, sugar and nuts, then milk and egg. Spoon mixture into prepared pan; sprinkle with combined extra sugar and extra cinnamon. Bake in moderately hot oven about 25 minutes.

MAKES 6
Per serving 21.9g fat; 1785kJ

38 lemon
sultana

sour cream muffins

1 cup (160g) sultanas

1 cup (250ml) boiling water

2½ cups (375g) self-raising flour

1 cup (220g) caster sugar

3 teaspoons finely grated lemon rind

90g butter, melted

¾ cup (180g) sour cream

½ cup (125ml) milk

2 eggs

Preheat oven to moderately hot. Grease 12-hole (⅓ cup/80ml) muffin pan.
Place sultanas and the water in medium heatproof bowl; stand 10 minutes. Drain sultanas, pat dry on absorbent paper.
Place flour in large bowl; stir in sultanas, sugar and rind, then combined remaining ingredients. Spoon mixture into prepared pan. Bake in moderately hot oven about 20 minutes.

MAKES 12
Per serving 13.8g fat; 1449kJ

40 passionfruit,
pineapple and mint muffins

You will need about four passionfruit for this recipe.

2 cups (300g)
self-raising flour

125g butter,
chopped coarsely

2/3 cup (150g)
caster sugar

2 tablespoons finely
chopped fresh mint

1/2 cup (115g) finely
chopped glacé
pineapple

1/4 cup (60ml)
passionfruit pulp

1/2 cup (125ml) cream

2 eggs, beaten lightly

yogurt cream

1/2 cup (125ml) cream

1/2 cup (140g) yogurt

1 teaspoon finely
grated orange rind

1 tablespoon
passionfruit pulp

Preheat oven to moderately hot. Grease 12-hole (1/3 cup/80ml) muffin pan.
Place flour in large bowl; rub in butter. Stir in sugar, mint, pineapple, passionfruit pulp, cream and egg. Spoon mixture into prepared pan. Bake in moderately hot oven about 20 minutes. Serve cold muffins filled with yogurt cream.
Yogurt Cream Beat cream and yogurt in small bowl with electric mixer until soft peaks form. Fold in rind and passionfruit pulp.

MAKES 12
Per serving 18.5g fat; 1401kJ

apple custard
muffins

1½ cups (225g)
self-raising flour

1 cup (160g)
wholemeal
self-raising flour

¼ cup (30g)
custard powder

1 teaspoon
ground cinnamon

½ cup (100g) firmly
packed brown sugar

2 egg whites

1 cup (250ml)
skim milk

¼ cup (60ml)
vegetable oil

410g can pie apples

¼ teaspoon ground
cinnamon, extra

2 teaspoons
caster sugar

Preheat oven to moderately hot. Grease
12-hole (⅓ cup/80ml) muffin pan, line with
paper muffin cases.

Sift flours, custard powder, cinnamon and brown
sugar into large bowl; stir in combined egg
whites, milk, oil and three-quarters of the pie
apple. Spoon mixture into prepared pan,
top with remaining pie apple; sprinkle with
combined extra cinnamon and caster sugar.
Bake in moderately hot oven about 30 minutes.

MAKES 12
Per serving 5.2g fat; 896kJ

triple chocolate
fudge muffins

2 cups (300g) self-raising flour

½ cup (50g) cocoa powder

1 cup (220g) caster sugar

1 egg, beaten lightly

90g butter, melted

¾ cup (180ml) buttermilk

½ cup (120g) sour cream

⅓ cup (65g) white Choc Bits

⅓ cup (65g) milk Choc Bits

⅓ cup (65g) dark Choc Bits

Preheat oven to moderate. Grease 12-hole (⅓ cup/80ml) muffin pan.
Sift dry ingredients into large bowl; stir in remaining ingredients. Spoon mixture into prepared pan. Bake in moderate oven about 25 minutes.

MAKES 12
Per serving 16.7g fat; 1488kJ

hazelnut, fig and
ricotta muffins

2¹/₂ cups (375g)
self-raising flour

90g butter,
chopped coarsely

³/₄ cup (150g) firmly
packed brown sugar

1 egg, beaten lightly

1¹/₄ cups (310ml)
buttermilk

filling

¹/₂ cup (95g) finely
chopped dried figs

¹/₄ cup (60ml) water

¹/₂ cup (100g)
ricotta cheese

¹/₄ cup (25g)
hazelnut meal

1 tablespoon
caster sugar

¹/₄ teaspoon
ground cinnamon

Preheat oven to moderately hot. Grease
six-hole (³/₄ cup/180ml) muffin pan.

Place flour in large bowl; rub in butter. Stir in
sugar, egg and buttermilk. Spoon half of the
muffin mixture into prepared pan, make a
well in each muffin, spoon in filling, top with
remaining muffin mixture. Bake in moderately
hot oven about 30 minutes.

Filling Combine figs and the water in small
saucepan. Bring to a boil; simmer, uncovered,
2 minutes, drain, cool. Combine figs with
remaining ingredients in small bowl.

MAKES 6
Per serving 20g fat; 2318kJ

carrot and

marmalade muffins

You will need about three medium carrots (360g) for this recipe.

1¹/₂ cups (225g) self-raising flour

1 cup (160g) wholemeal self-raising flour

¹/₂ teaspoon bicarbonate of soda

¹/₂ cup (100g) firmly packed brown sugar

¹/₃ cup (55g) sultanas

¹/₃ cup (40g) finely chopped walnuts

1¹/₂ cups finely grated, firmly packed carrot

¹/₂ cup (170g) marmalade, warmed

100g butter, melted

¹/₂ cup (125ml) milk

2 eggs, beaten lightly

2 tablespoons marmalade, warmed, extra

¹/₄ cup (30g) finely chopped walnuts, extra

Preheat oven to moderately hot. Grease 12-hole (¹/₃ cup/80ml) muffin pan.

Sift flours, soda and sugar into large bowl, stir in sultanas, nuts, carrot and marmalade, then combined butter, milk and eggs. Spoon mixture into prepared pan. Bake in moderately hot oven about 25 minutes. Turn muffins onto wire rack; top with extra marmalade and nuts.

MAKES 12
Per serving 12g fat; 1314kJ

lamington

muffins

2¹/₂ cups (375g) self-raising flour

³/₄ cup (165g) caster sugar

2 teaspoons vanilla essence

1 egg

125g butter, melted

¹/₂ cup (125ml) milk

¹/₄ cup (60ml) cream

¹/₄ cup (20g) desiccated coconut

chocolate frosting

¹/₄ cup (60ml) cream

50g dark chocolate, chopped coarsely

30g butter

1 cup (160g) icing sugar mixture

Preheat oven to moderately hot. Grease 10 holes (¹/₃ cup/80ml) of a muffin pan. Combine flour and sugar in large bowl; stir in combined essence, egg, butter, milk and cream. Spoon mixture into prepared pan. Bake in moderately hot oven about 20 minutes. Spread top of cold muffins with chocolate frosting; sprinkle with coconut.

Chocolate Frosting Combine cream, chocolate and butter in small saucepan; stir over heat, without boiling, until chocolate melts. Remove pan from heat, gradually beat in icing sugar. Cover; refrigerate 5 minutes, stirring occasionally, until a spreading consistency.

MAKES 10
Per serving 22.2g fat; 1956kJ

48 oat bran,

banana and pecan muffins

You will need about two large overripe bananas (460g) for this recipe.

³/₄ cup (120g) wholemeal self-raising flour

1 cup (150g) white self-raising flour

¹/₂ teaspoon mixed spice

2 tablespoons brown sugar

¹/₂ cup (60g) oat bran

¹/₂ cup (60g) finely chopped pecans

1 cup mashed bananas

¹/₄ cup (60ml) vegetable oil

2 eggs

¹/₃ cup (80ml) skim milk

2 tablespoons honey

12 pecans, extra

Preheat oven to moderately hot. Grease 12-hole (¹/₃ cup/80ml) muffin pan.
Sift flours, spice and sugar into large bowl; stir in oat bran and chopped nuts, then combined banana, oil, eggs, milk and honey. Spoon mixture into prepared pan; top with extra nuts.
Bake in moderately hot oven about 20 minutes.

MAKES 12
Per serving
11.4g fat; 994kJ

frosted carrot and orange muffins

You will need about three medium carrots (360g) for this recipe.

2 cups (300g)
self-raising flour

¹/₂ cup (80g)
wholemeal
plain flour

¹/₂ cup (110g) caster
sugar

1¹/₂ cups finely
grated, firmly
packed carrot

2 eggs

125g butter, melted

¹/₂ cup (125ml) milk

1 teaspoon finely
grated orange rind

¹/₂ cup (125ml)
orange juice

frosting

250g cream cheese

¹/₄ cup (40g) icing
sugar mixture

2 teaspoons finely
grated orange rind

Preheat oven to
moderately hot.
Grease 12-hole
(¹/₃ cup/80ml)
muffin pan.
Sift flours and sugar
into large bowl;
stir in combined
carrot, eggs, butter,
milk, rind and juice.
Spoon mixture into
prepared pan.
Bake in moderately
hot oven about
25 minutes.
Spread cold muffins
with frosting, top
with glacé orange
rind, if desired.
Frosting Beat
cheese, icing sugar
and rind in small
bowl with electric
mixer until smooth.

MAKES 12
Per serving
17.2g fat; 1366kJ

hazelnut
passionfruit muffins

2 cups (300g) self-raising flour

1 teaspoon mixed spice

80g butter, chopped coarsely

1 cup (110g) hazelnut meal

1 cup (220g) caster sugar

1 egg, beaten lightly

3/4 cup (180ml) milk

filling

170g can passionfruit in syrup

1 1/2 tablespoons caster sugar

2 tablespoons water

1 tablespoon cornflour

Preheat oven to moderately hot. Grease six-hole (3/4 cup/180ml) muffin pan.
Combine flour and spice in large bowl; rub in butter. Stir in hazelnut meal and sugar then egg and milk. Spoon mixture into prepared pan, make a well in each muffin, spoon in filling. Bake in moderately hot oven about 25 minutes.
Filling Combine passionfruit and sugar in small saucepan, stir in blended water and cornflour; stir over heat until mixture boils and thickens, cool 5 minutes.

MAKES 6
Per serving 25g fat; 2464kJ

basic muffins

To make the banana walnut variation, you will need two large overripe bananas (460g).

2 cups (300g)
self-raising flour

1 cup (150g) plain flour

1 teaspoon bicarbonate
of soda

1 cup (200g) firmly
packed brown sugar

2 eggs

1½ cups (375ml) milk

¾ cup (180ml) vegetable oil

apple cinnamon

2 teaspoons
ground cinnamon

1½ cups (210g) finely
chopped apple

blueberry

200g fresh or frozen
blueberries

banana walnut

1 cup mashed
overripe banana

1 cup (120g) finely
chopped walnuts

topping

¼ cup (50g) firmly
packed brown sugar

¼ cup (35g) plain flour

40g butter

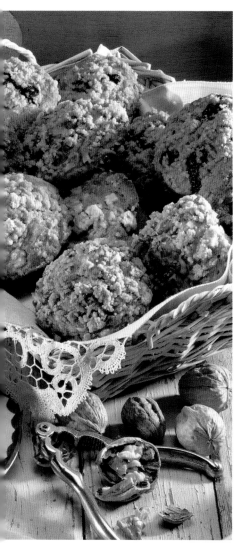

Preheat oven to moderately hot. Grease 16 holes (1/3 cup/80ml) of two muffin pans.

Sift dry ingredients into large bowl; stir in combined eggs, milk and oil. Add ingredients for your chosen variation, following methods given. Bake in moderately hot oven about 20 minutes.

Apple Cinnamon Sift cinnamon with dry ingredients; stir in 1 cup of the apple. Sprinkle muffins with remaining apple and Topping.

Blueberry Spoon half of the basic muffin mixture into prepared pans; sprinkle with half of the blueberries, spoon over remaining mixture. Sprinkle with remaining blueberries and Topping.

Banana Walnut Stir banana and half of the walnuts into basic muffin mixture. Sprinkle muffins with remaining walnuts and Topping.

Topping Combine sugar and flour in small bowl; rub in butter.

MAKES 16
Per serving:
apple cinnamon 14.4g fat; 1264kJ
blueberry 14.4g fat; 1264kJ
banana walnut 19.5g fat; 1505kJ

54 moist
coconut
chocolate-chip muffins

2¹/₂ cups (375g) self-raising flour

¹/₂ cup (45g) desiccated coconut

³/₄ cup (165g) caster sugar

90g butter, melted

¹/₂ cup (120g) sour cream

¹/₄ cup (60ml) milk

2 eggs

¹/₂ cup (95g) milk Choc Bits

2 tablespoons milk Choc Bits, extra

Preheat oven to moderate. Grease six-hole (³/₄ cup/180ml) muffin pan. **Combine** flour, coconut and sugar in large bowl; stir in combined butter, cream, milk and eggs, then Choc Bits. Spoon mixture into prepared pan, top with extra Choc Bits. Bake in moderate oven about 25 minutes.

MAKES 6
Per serving 34g fat; 2870kJ

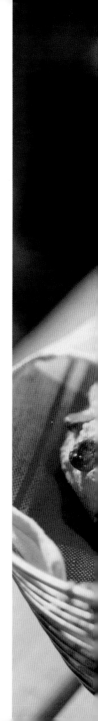

56   hazelnut plum muffins

90g butter, melted

2¹/₂ cups (375g)
self-raising flour

¹/₂ cup (55g)
hazelnut meal

²/₃ cup (150g)
caster sugar

1 egg, beaten lightly

1 cup (250ml) milk

¹/₂ cup (160g)
plum jam

Preheat oven to
moderately hot. Grease
12-hole (¹/₃ cup/80ml)
muffin pan.

Combine butter, flour,
hazelnut meal, sugar,
egg and milk in large
bowl. Spoon half of
the muffin mixture into
prepared pan, make
a well in each muffin,
spoon in rounded
teaspoons of jam, top
with remaining muffin
mixture. Bake in
moderately hot oven
about 20 minutes.

MAKES 12
Per serving
10.6g fat; 1212kJ

apricot coconut muffins

2 cups (300g)
self-raising flour

125g butter,
chopped coarsely

³/₄ cup (165g)
caster sugar

1 cup (150g)
dried apricots,
chopped finely

1 cup (90g)
desiccated coconut

³/₄ cup (180ml) milk

2 eggs, beaten lightly

Preheat oven to moderately hot. Grease 12-hole (¹/₃ cup/80ml) muffin pan.
Place flour in large bowl; rub in butter. Stir in remaining ingredients. Spoon mixture into prepared pan. Bake in moderately hot oven about 20 minutes.

MAKES 12
Per serving
15.2g fat; 1283kJ

spiced apple and rhubarb muffins

3 cups (450g) self-raising flour

1 cup (200g) firmly packed brown sugar

1 teaspoon ground cinnamon

1 teaspoon mixed spice

125g butter, chopped coarsely

3/4 cup (180ml) buttermilk

2 eggs

1/2 x 410g can pie apples

2 cups (220g) finely chopped rhubarb

2 teaspoons cinnamon sugar

Preheat oven to moderately hot. Grease 12-hole (1/3 cup/80ml) muffin pan.
Sift flour, brown sugar and spices into large bowl; rub in butter. Stir in combined milk and eggs, then apple and rhubarb. Spoon mixture into prepared pan; sprinkle with cinnamon sugar. Bake in moderately hot oven about 20 minutes.

MAKES 12
Per serving 10.3g fat; 1246kJ

glossary

almonds, flaked almonds cut into paper-thin slices.

baking powder a raising agent consisting mainly of two parts cream of tartar to one part bicarbonate of soda (baking soda).

gluten free: a raising agent based on rice flour; available from health food shops.

bicarbonate of soda also known as baking or carb soda.

bran

oat: outer layer of oat grain.

rice: outer layer of rice grain.

wheat: outer layer of wheat grain.

butter use salted or unsalted ("sweet") butter; 125g is equal to one stick butter.

buttermilk (contains 1.8g fat per 100ml) sold alongside fresh milk products; despite the implication of its name, is low in fat. Originally the liquid left after butter was churned; today, it is commercially made similarly to yogurt. A good lower-fat substitution for dairy products like cream or sour cream; good in baking and salad dressings.

chocolate

choc bits: also known as chocolate chips and chocolate morsels; available in milk, white and dark chocolate. Made of cocoa butter, cocoa liquor, sugar and an emulsifier, these hold their shape in baking and are ideal for decorating.

chocolate orange thins: thin chocolates with orange-flavoured filling; any thin pieces of chocolate can be used.

cocoa powder: substance left after cocoa butter is extracted from chocolate mass and powdered.

dark: eating chocolate; made of cocoa butter, a high proportion of cocoa liquor (solids), and sugar.

white: eating chocolate, basically cocoa butter – without any cocoa liquor (solids) – sugar and milk.

coconut

desiccated: unsweetened, concentrated, dried shredded coconut.

flaked: flaked and dried coconut flesh.

shredded: thin strips of dried coconut.

cornflour also known as cornstarch; used as a thickening agent in cooking.

cream (minimum fat content 35%) also known as pure cream and pouring cream; containing no additives like commercially thickened cream.

sour: (minimum fat content 35%) a thick, commercially cultured soured cream good for dips, toppings and baked cheesecakes.

cream cheese soft milk cheese commonly known as Philadelphia or Philly.

custard powder packaged, powdered mixture of starch (wheat or corn), artificial flavouring and colouring agents that can be used to eliminate eggs. Sometimes sold in packages as vanilla pudding mixture.

essence also known as extracts; generally the byproduct of distillation of plants.

flour

brown rice: made from ground whole-grain brown rice.

plain: all-purpose flour, made from wheat.

self-raising: plain flour sifted with baking powder in the proportion of 1 cup flour to 2 teaspoons baking powder.

soy: made from ground soy beans.

wholemeal self-raising flour: wholemeal flour sifted with baking powder.

grand marnier an orange-flavoured brandy-based liqueur.

hazelnut meal hazelnuts ground to a fine, flour-like texture.

jam also known as preserve or conserve; most often made from fruit.

maple-flavoured syrup also known as golden or pancake syrup but not a substitute for pure maple syrup.

milk we used full-cream homogenised milk unless otherwise specified in recipes.

evaporated: unsweetened canned milk from which water has been extracted by evaporation.

skim: we used milk with 0.1% fat content.

soy: a non-dairy drink; made from ground, cooked soy beans.

mixed dried fruit a combination of sultanas, raisins, currants, mixed peel and cherries.

mixed spice a blend of ground spices usually consisting of cinnamon, allspice and nutmeg.

muesli crunchy granola.

nutella chocolate hazelnut spread; available in supermarkets.

oil, vegetable any of a number of oils sourced from plants rather than animal fats.

pumpkin also known as squash; we used butternut pumpkin in these recipes unless specified otherwise.

raisins dried sweet grapes.

rhubarb a vegetable; only the firm reddish stems are eaten.

ricotta cheese sweet, fairly moist, fresh curd cheese having a low fat content.

rum, dark liquor made from fermented sugar cane; we used an underproof rum (not overproof) for its subtle flavour.

sugar

brown: a soft fine sugar retaining molasses.

caster: also known as superfine or finely granulated table sugar.

cinnamon sugar: combination of ground cinnamon and caster sugar.

icing sugar mixture: also known as confectioners' sugar or powdered sugar; granulated sugar crushed together with a small amount (about 3%) cornflour added.

raw: natural brown granulated sugar.

sultanas small dried grapes, also known as golden raisins.

yogurt we used plain unflavoured yogurt.

conversion chart

MEASURES

One Australian metric measuring cup holds approximately 250ml, one Australian metric tablespoon holds 20ml, one Australian metric teaspoon holds 5ml.

The difference between one country's measuring cups and another's is within a two- or three-teaspoon variance, and will not affect your cooking results. North America, New Zealand and the United Kingdom use a 15ml tablespoon.

All cup and spoon measurements are level. The most accurate way of measuring dry ingredients is to weigh them. When measuring liquids, use a clear glass or plastic jug with the metric markings.

We use large eggs with an average weight of 60g.

DRY MEASURES

METRIC	IMPERIAL
15g	½oz
30g	1oz
60g	2oz
90g	3oz
125g	4oz (¼lb)
155g	5oz
185g	6oz
220g	7oz
250g	8oz (½lb)
280g	9oz
315g	10oz
345g	11oz
375g	12oz (¾lb)
410g	13oz
440g	14oz
470g	15oz
500g	16oz (1lb)
750g	24oz (1½lb)
1kg	32oz (2lb)

LIQUID MEASURES

METRIC	IMPERIAL
30ml	1 fluid oz
60ml	2 fluid oz
100ml	3 fluid oz
125ml	4 fluid oz
150ml	5 fluid oz (¼ pint/1 gill)
190ml	6 fluid oz
250ml	8 fluid oz
300ml	10 fluid oz (½ pint)
500ml	16 fluid oz
600ml	20 fluid oz (1 pint)
1000ml (1 litre)	1¾ pints

LENGTH MEASURES

METRIC	IMPERIAL
3mm	⅛in
6mm	¼in
1cm	½in
2cm	¾in
2.5cm	1in
5cm	2in
6cm	2½in
8cm	3in
10cm	4in
13cm	5in
15cm	6in
18cm	7in
20cm	8in
23cm	9in
25cm	10in
28cm	11in
30cm	12in (1ft)

OVEN TEMPERATURES

These oven temperatures are only a guide for conventional ovens. For fan-forced ovens, check the manufacturer's manual.

	°C (CELSIUS)	°F (FAHRENHEIT)	GAS MARK
Very slow	120	250	½
Slow	150	275 – 300	1 – 2
Moderately slow	160	325	3
Moderate	180	350 – 375	4 – 5
Moderately hot	200	400	6
Hot	220	425 – 450	7 – 8
Very hot	240	475	9

index

Published in 2001 by Bauer Media Books, Sydney
Bauer Media Books are published by Bauer Media Limited
54 Park St, Sydney
GPO Box 4088, Sydney, NSW 2001.
phone (02) 9282 8618; fax (02) 9126 3702
www.awwcookbooks.com.au

MEDIA GROUP

BAUER MEDIA BOOKS
Publishing Director – Gerry Reynolds
Publisher – Sally Wright
Editorial & Food Director – Pamela Clark
Creative Director – Hieu Chi Nguyen
Food Concept Director – Sophia Young
Director of Sales, Marketing & Rights – Brian Cearnes

Published and Distributed in the United Kingdom by Octopus Publishing Group
Endeavour House
189 Shaftesbury Avenue
London WC2H 8JY
United Kingdom
phone (+44)(0)207 632 5400; fax (+44)(0)207 632 5405
info@octopus-publishing.co.uk;
www.octopusbooks.co.uk

To order books:
telephone LBS on 01903 828 503
order online at
www.australian-womens-weekly.com
or www.octopusbooks.co.uk

Printed in Thailand
International foreign language rights, Brian Cearnes, Bauer Media Books
bcearnes@bauer-media.com.au

A catalogue record for this book is available from the British Library.
ISBN 978-1-90742-893-7
© Bauer Media Limited 2001
ABN 18 053 273 546

Cover White chocolate and berry muffins, page 34
Photographer – Stuart Scott
Stylist – Anna Phillips